SUPER CHAMPIONS OF ICE HOCKEY

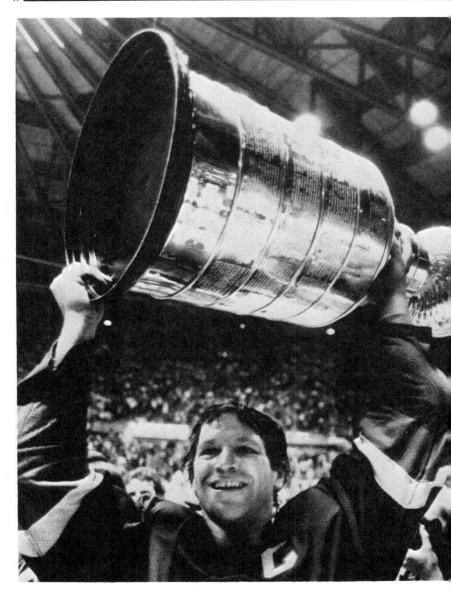

In this moment of triumph in 1982, Denis Potvin, captain of the New York Islanders, holds high the Stanley Cup. His team just defeated the Vancouver Canucks to retain the great trophy.

WINNERS!

SUPER CHAMPIONS OF ICE HOCKEY

ROSS R. OLNEY

Illustrated with photographs

CLARION BOOKS

TICKNOR & FIELDS: A HOUGHTON MIFFLIN COMPANY

NEW YORK

TO BRUCE, JOE, JAYNE, MIKE,

AND THE OTHERS IN CORNERS AT THE FORUM

CLARION BOOKS
TICKNOR & FIELDS, A HOUGHTON MIFFLIN COMPANY
Copyright © 1982 by Ross R. Olney

Printed in the United States of America

LIBRARY OF CONGRESS CATALOGING IN PUBLICATION DATA
Olney, Ross Robert, 1929–
    Super-champions of ice hockey.
    (Winners!)
    Summary: Profiles the super champions
of ice hockey and explains how the sport is
played professionally.
    1. Hockey—Juvenile literature.
2. Hockey players—Biography—Juvenile literature.
[1. Hockey players.   2. Hockey]   I. Title.   II. Series.
GV847.25.046   796.96′2′0922 [B] [920]   82-1310

V 10 9 8 7 6 5 4 3 2 1

ISBN 0-89919-109-6   AACR2

ACKNOWLEDGMENTS

The author wishes to thank the following for photos, advice and information about the players in this book.

John Halligan, New York Rangers
Jayne Kamin, photographer
Claude Mouton, Montreal Canadiens
Bruce L. Schwartzman, photographer
Bill Tuele, Edmonton Oilers
Scott Vlha, photographer
and especially Scott Carmichael of the
Los Angeles Kings and Bill Libby, author of many
exciting hockey stories.
Thanks also to my son, Scott Olney,
for all the darkroom work.

All photographs are by Ross R. Olney except for the following, which are used through the courtesty of: Hockey Hall of Fame, 4–5; Jayne Kamin, 44, 48; Montreal Canadiens, 88, 89; National Hockey League, 29, 74, 75; New York Islanders, 13, 60, 61; New York Rangers, 102, 103, 105; 97th Street Camera, 45; Bruce L. Schwartzman, 83; United Press International, facing title page; Scott Vlha, 2, 10, 28, 41, 66, 67, 71, 114, 115.

CONTENTS

INTRODUCTION

Ice hockey is a hard, tough game.

Hockey players strap razor-sharp blades to their feet. They carry a big stick. They use *both*. Usually to get the puck into the goal. But sometimes on each other.

Hockey is easy to understand. The idea is to get the puck into the goal net. There are five men on each team to do it. Three are *forwards* who do most of the shooting. Two are *defensemen* who try to keep the other team from shooting. Also, sometimes the defensemen shoot the puck at the enemy goal.

That's five.

There is a sixth player on each team, a *goaltender*. Most hockey fans call this player a *goalie*. Padded with equipment, he stands in front of the

The forwards do most of the shooting. Here Charlie Simmer (*right*) of the Los Angeles Kings scores against Mike Liut of the St. Louis Blues.

goal. He tries to block the shots. He tries to keep the puck from going into his goal.

The goalies are the last line of defense for each team.

Before hockey goalies began to wear masks to protect their face, they were often badly hurt. Many goaltenders had scars all over their face. One goalie had more than six hundred stitches in his face and head alone.

It is still a tough position to play. But National Hockey League goalies are tough people.

Hockey is a very colorful game. Imagine all the colors of the rainbow in the uniforms of the players. Two teams line up for the start of the game. They are splashes of bright color on the white ice.

The referee drops the puck between two of the forwards and the game is on. This puck dropping is called a *face-off*. Each team tries to get the puck into the enemy team's goal.

How do they get it into the goal?

The puck can be *shot* in.

It can be glanced in, off another player. Or off the goal posts.

It can even be bounced in off the goalie.

It can be shot in from close up, or from far away. If shot from far away, it is usually called a *slap shot*.

If the puck is near the goal, it might go in after a wild flurry of action. A red light snaps on. A siren screams. The crowd roars. A player stabs his stick high into the air in triumph. The others on his team leap on him. They pound on his back in glee.

Defensemen also score. This was a game-winning goal by Bruins' defenseman Bobby Orr in a playoff game. He was tripped but still scored.

He has managed one of the hardest scores in all of sports.

The players on a hockey team are lined up like this. The three forwards are called *center, right wing* and *left wing.* These three generally score most of the goals. They go up the ice toward the enemy first. One of the forwards is in the center of the ice and one is down each side. They try to get the puck into the goal.

Behind them come two defensemen. They hang back in case the puck changes hands. The defensemen guard their own goal. They only go up the ice toward the enemy when the puck has been moved forward, away from their own goal.

There have been some high-scoring defensemen. But not too often. The great Bobby Orr was a defenseman who scored many goals. The right and left defensemen are allowed to shoot the puck. But they usually take long slap shots from out away from the goal.

The ice rink is divided into three equal sections by *blue lines*. This makes a *defensive zone* near a team's own goal. There is a *neutral zone* in the center. There is an *attacking* or *offensive zone* near the enemy goal. This is reversed for the other team coming the other way.

There is also a *red line* that cuts the ice into two equal parts. The face-off to start each of the three periods of a game is held at the center, red line.

Each period of a hockey game is twenty minutes long. So a game is one hour long. There are rest periods between each playing period.

Three officials are on the ice. Several more officials are off the ice for each game. On the ice, the *referee* controls the game. He calls the penalties. He is assisted by two *linesmen* who watch for special problems.

Off the ice are *goal judges* for each goal. They turn on the light and siren if a puck goes into the goal. They are needed because sometimes the puck bounces in and out very quickly. You can see the goal judge at every hockey game. He sits behind the glass just to the rear of the goal. The judge is watching the goal very closely. He has a button in his hand to light the light and start the siren.

In one game a puck split in half. One half went in the goal; the other half missed. No goal was allowed. The judges said the thing that went into the net was not the official shape and size of a puck. No real puck went into the goal, so there could be no goal.

There are other officials off the ice. There is an official in each *penalty box*. The others are time-keeping and scoring officials.

The referee calls penalties and sends players to the penalty box. They can be sent there for a certain period of time. Most fans quickly learn the penalties if they go to a hockey game. While a player is in the penalty box, his team must play short-handed, without him, until the time ends. Meanwhile, the other team is on a *power play*. This means it has one more man on the ice than the penalized team.

The minor (two-minute) penalties include the following:

1. *Tripping* another player
2. *Holding* another player with your arms

3. *Slashing* another player with your stick
4. *Charging* into another player after a running start
5. *Hooking* another player with your stick
6. *Interfering* with another player's movement
7. *Falling on the puck* on purpose
8. *Cross-checking,* or hitting another player with your stick.

Fighting is not allowed, either. The referee can send a player into the penalty box for a longer period of time for fighting. The player can even be sent out of the game. Of course, hockey players often take a chance and fight anyhow.

There are three other hockey terms most fans learn about.

Icing is when the game is delayed by a player's shooting the puck all the way down the ice. If the puck goes over from the player's own side of the red line to the enemy goal line (but not into the goal), it is icing. Into the goal would be a *score,* of course.

Offside is when a player goes over the enemy blue line before the puck goes over it.

An *offside pass* is when the puck is passed

across *two* of the lines on the ice. Players are not allowed to pass the puck that far forward.

If any of these three things happens in a game (and they do very often) the referee calls for a new face-off. But the face-off is not held at center ice. This time it is held nearer the goal of the team who was caught doing one of them.

Don't let all these rules or penalties confuse you and turn you away from hockey. It is a bright, colorful, fast, exciting game. The action never stops unless there is a penalty or a serious injury. Even the substitution of players is done "on the fly," with the game going right on. You will learn the simple rules and penalties as you go.

Meanwhile, the idea is to enjoy the game. Just watch each team try to force the puck into the enemy goal. Watch each coach try to out-think the other with player substitutions. Watch the defensemen try to keep the star forwards from scoring. Watch the goalie leap and twist and sprawl to block the puck.

The team gets one point for each goal it scores. The team with the most goals wins. Or the game can end in a tie. Only in the Stanley Cup playoffs, the championship series, are ties not allowed. The teams keep playing period after period until one wins. Some Stanley Cup games have gone on for *hours*.

The players also have a point system of their own. This has nothing to do with who wins or loses the game. Players get one point for a goal and one point for an assist. The player who actually puts the puck in the net gets a point for the

The goalies are the last line of defense. Marcel Dionne (*front*) of the Kings slips by a defenseman. He scores against the New York Rangers' goalie.

goal. Then the last two players to help by passing the puck, or even touching it, get one point each for an assist.

Players try to get the most points each season. Those players who get many points usually get a raise in pay. They also get trophies and other awards for being high-scoring players.

This book has more forwards than defensemen or goalies. The forwards are the ones who usually score goals. The forwards in this book are Mike Bossy, Wayne Gretzky, Phil Esposito, Guy Lafleur and Marcel Dionne. Defensemen are very important to a team, but they don't usually score too many goals. They usually keep the *other* team from scoring goals. The defenseman in this book is Denis Potvin. He is one of the best in the NHL.

Goalies are very famous in hockey. The goalie is often the most famous player on the team. The goalie in this book was very famous *before* he became a pro hockey player. He was an American hero, in fact. Now he is playing in the National Hockey League.

He is Jim Craig, the goalie for the amazing American hockey team that won a gold medal in the 1980 Olympic Games.

ONE

MIKE BOSSY

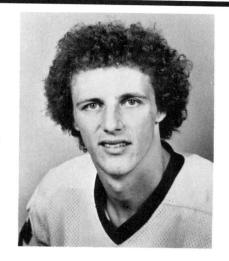

No player had scored 50 goals in 50 games since Maurice ("Rocket") Richard. Nobody thought it could ever be done again. Richard was one of the greatest goal-scoring players in the history of hockey. He had set his record in the 1944–45 hockey season.

But in 1981 one player was getting very close. He was Mike Bossy of the New York Islanders. Bossy is one of the greatest modern players in the sport.

Most of the NHL forwards say Bossy's wrist shot is frightening. He barely flicks his wrists as

Opposite: Mike Bossy is one of the smoothest skaters in hockey. Here he bores into enemy territory. He knows the puck will be passed to him at the right instant.

he twitches his stick. The puck goes speeding straight between the keeper's legs. Or over his shoulder into a high corner of the goal. Or out to one side, just out of the goalie's reach.

Bossy is a thrilling player to watch. The Islanders, with his help, won the Stanley Cup in 1980. They were the champions. And in 1981 they were well on their way to another Stanley Cup. Mostly because of Mike Bossy's goals.

Bossy was averaging a goal every game. In 50 games, he *could* get 50 goals. He could if he could keep his "string" going.

But then, with 48 goals in 48 games, his scoring streak stopped. It stopped *cold*.

Meanwhile, one other player was trying for the same record that year, Charlie Simmer of the Los Angeles Kings. He had scored 46 goals going into his fiftieth game. In game number 50, Simmer managed to score three goals, a *hat trick!*

That gave him 49 goals. A fine goal-scoring pace, but not quite up to Richard's record.

Bossy still had a chance until his goal scoring seemed to stop. He couldn't get off a shot. The other teams were blocking every attempt. Sometimes two defensemen would hound him. Sometimes the other team had *three* players guarding him. He didn't seem to have a chance.

That's how it is in pro sports. Nobody wants a player to set a record at *his* expense. So every team the Islanders played guarded Bossy very closely.

To make matters worse, Bossy missed two shots at an empty net in his forty-eighth game. Those shots would have given him the record in two fewer games than Richard had scored his 50 games, 50 goals record. But Bossy had missed.

Players can get shots into an empty net if the enemy goalie has been called to the bench. Suppose your team is behind by one goal. Suppose there is only a minute or two left to play. You might decide to pull your goalie out of the game. This gives you the chance to send in another player to try to score. So you send in a good shooting forward. He may tie the game for you with a goal. At the enemy end of the ice, your team would have a one-man advantage.

But at *your* end of the ice, the net stands empty. The enemy team might get control of the puck and bring it down the ice. Then they have an easy shot.

Coaches who pull goalies feel that it is no worse to lose a game by two goals than by one goal. And it could help the team to tie the score. A tie in hockey is much better than a loss. A tie gives the team one point in the standings. A win gives the team two points. A loss gives them no points at all.

But Bossy had missed two empty-net shots. Then it was game number 50. He had 48 goals. He needed two goals to match Richard's record. He kept trying and trying. But the other team, the Quebec Nordiques, guarded him carefully.

Finally, at last, Bossy scored a goal. He had 49 goals. He needed only one more. But it didn't look good. The game was nearly over.

Then Bossy skimmed down the left side of the rink. He skidded to a stop in a spray of ice. At that instant, across the ice, his teammate Clark Gillies had the puck. Gillies saw his pal and fired a quick pass. Bossy was open and the puck headed for his stick.

Goalie Ron Grahame braced himself for the shot he knew was coming. He seemed coiled like a snake. He was ready to move in any direction. Bossy's teammates shouted at him to *shoot!*

"My teammates were really pumping me up,"

he later recalled. "I kept telling myself that the moment I had been dreaming about for so long was right there, *now.*"

Bossy's wrists jerked and the puck zipped away just as it touched his stick. Grahame moved quickly, but he was too late. The puck skimmed between his leg pads and into the back of the net.

"I did it! I did it!" shouted Bossy with a huge grin on his face. He had matched the great Rocket Richard's record. "It's so incredible," Bossy told the cheering crowd.

One hockey coach was asked what gift he wanted for Christmas. "A Mike Bossy doll," he said. "You just wind it up and it scores 60 goals a year." It is tough to score goals but the coach thought Bossy made it look easy.

Mike Bossy is a quiet man. He doesn't *act* like a sports hero. He avoids crowds and publicity. He is a family man. He prefers being with his wife, Lucie, and his young daughter Josiane. To him, hockey is a job. It is the way he earns his living.

Bossy is against violence in hockey. Often players will drop their gloves and start hitting each other. Not Mike Bossy. Although he takes a great deal of punishment from other players on the ice, he doesn't believe in fighting. He doesn't believe fighting should be a part of hockey, as it now is. He has said he will never drop his gloves to fight.

He out-skates and out-shoots his opponents. He doesn't believe he should have to fight them, too.

Fans say they only really see Bossy when he is scoring. Otherwise, he is a ghost on the ice, appearing here and there for just an instant. One coach said, "I thought our guys did a pretty good job of checking [guarding] Bossy tonight. He only touched the puck about half a dozen times."

The trouble was, Mike Bossy got *four goals* in that same game.

He scored two goals in the 1982 All-Star Game against one of the best goalies in the business, Gilles Meloche of Minnesota. One of these was an exciting *breakaway* score, where a player skates in alone. Bossy slipped around all-star defenseman Larry Robinson of the Montreal Canadiens and fired the puck past the goalie and into the net.

He was chosen Most Valuable Player of the all-star game that year.

Only a month later, with 299 goals to his credit during his career, Bossy and the Islanders were

Mike Bossy, who wears number 22, is dumped hard by enemy player number 22. Flattening someone is legal in hockey, so players often go for the other team's super-champion.

playing the Washington Capitals. Of course every hockey player would like to reach the 300-goal mark, but not many do. Bossy did. He made *sure* by scoring *four* goals during that one game.

For the third time in five years, Bossy had scored at least 60 goals per season. The only other player in NHL history to score 60 or more goals more than once was Phil Esposito, who did it four times. Chances are, Bossy will catch Phil before he is through playing.

Mike Bossy's parents, Dorothy and Bordon Bossy, had ten children. Mike was the fifth. He has five brothers and four sisters. He was a star in Canadian junior hockey. In fact, he met his future wife, Lucie, at a hockey rink. She was working in a concession stand and he was playing. Mike was fourteen years old.

When he signed with the Islanders, they were married. That was on July 23, 1977. He has been an NHL star from that day on.

Oddly, Bossy was not the young player selected first during his draft year. *Drafting* is when pro teams pick players from the amateur teams. Of course, the very best players are usually picked first. Several teams passed over Bossy for other players. Now, many coaches and owners think they know why. For one thing, they felt he wasn't all that good on defense. And for another, as a goal shooter he was simply "too good to be true." They felt that *nobody* could play as well as Mike Bossy was playing in the juniors. They believed that he was a *flash in the pan*. They thought he would fall apart as soon as he played against pro players.

But he didn't. Not by a *long shot.*

Bossy was finally drafted by the Islanders. He has played there ever since.

"When I score a goal, the feeling I get is something I'd wish on people," says Bossy with a grin.

During a game Bossy cruises in slow circles back and forth through the *slot* out in front of the goal. Then the puck is shot out to Bossy from one of the rink's corners. Instantly, with blinding speed, Bossy fires at the net. He doesn't give the goalie time to get set. Often, the goalie doesn't even *see* the puck.

Phil Esposito, another great goal scorer, was telling *Sports Illustrated* magazine about Bossy. "Mike may not even realize it, but he's absolutely relentless in his pursuit of a goal."

Tony Esposito is Phil's brother, and a famous goalie for the Chicago Black Hawks. He told *Time* magazine, "Bossy has the knack of hitting the open spot in the net, just like my brother Phil. You can't teach that. You have to be born with that instinct for the spot where the goalie isn't."

Bossy, number 22 in the rear, seldom fights on the ice. Instead, he uses his strength and skill to score goals.

Bossy plays right wing on the Islanders. When Bossy joined the team, he was put on a line with Bryan Trottier and Clark Gillies. It was the top line of the team. These were the best scorers. Some of the other Islanders who had been on the team much longer were jealous. That didn't bother Bossy. He started shooting just as he had been doing in the juniors.

Very soon he also became one of the top scorers

in the big leagues. He scored 53 goals the very first year. That is still a record for a rookie player. The next year he scored 69 goals. He was amazing.

In pro hockey officials keep dozens of records. One record names the top scorers overall, in hockey history. They figure this by counting the number of games the player was in. Then they count the number of goals he scored. This gives a percentage figure.

The great Guy Lafleur, for example, is in fifth place with .594. That means he scores in more than half the games he plays in. A *fine* record. Phil Esposito ranks in fourth place at .621. In third place is Babe Dye. He played for Toronto from 1919 to 1930. He averaged a solid .738. In second place overall is Cy Denneny. Denneny played for the Ottawa Senators and the Boston Bruins from 1917 to 1929.

Denneny scored 250 goals in only 326 games for a solid .767 percentage.

By the middle of the 1981–82 season (the hockey season runs through Christmas and New Year's), the twenty-three-year-old Bossy had scored 303 goals. In 381 games. That made his percentage .795. That was the best in the history of hockey to that time.

Professional hockey players are *tough*. Bossy may not choose to fight, but he is one of the toughest. He doesn't believe in giving up. Injury doesn't stop him.

During the 1981 Stanley Cup finals, Bossy's line was on the ice. He was streaking down the boards with the puck when a New York Ranger defenseman *flattened* him. Bossy went down, and out. He fell as though he had been shot. His face was bloody.

The game went on as Bossy struggled to the bench. Towels were used to stop the blood and clean up Bossy's face. Still dazed and staggering, he then insisted on returning to the game. There were only a few seconds left in the period. He could have left the game for good. Or at least he could have rested between periods.

Instead, he skated back onto the ice for the final few seconds.

"You've got to get back up," he told the New York *Daily News*. "If they're gonna hit you, they're gonna hit you. But you *get back up*."

The 1982 Stanley Cup playoffs were a series of

Bossy is dumped by Kings' defenseman Rick
Chartraw in a game in Los Angeles.

"dream games" for Mike Bossy and his teammates. They rushed through the semifinal series,
polishing off their opponents in four straight
games. In the finals, against the Vancouver Canucks, they also played only four games of a possible seven.

In the first game of the finals Mike Bossy stole a pass in overtime and scored a game-ending goal. The Islanders went on to win. In the third game he shot a backhanded goal while he was flying through the air. This goal doubled the Islanders' lead. In the fourth game he scored two power-play goals, including the game-winning goal.

The Islanders had become only the third team in NHL history to win the Stanley Cup at least three times in a row. The other two teams were the mighty Montreal Canadiens and the Toronto Maple Leafs.

And Mike Bossy? He tied the great Jean Beliveau of the Canadiens for most goals in a final round of the Stanley Cup (7). Best of all next to winning the great silver cup, Mike Bossy was awarded the Conn Smythe Trophy as the Most Valuable Player in the playoffs.

Mike Bossy is one of hockey's best goal scorers. He is also a "team player."

Bossy had scored his fiftieth goal in 50 games. In the last few seconds of that fiftieth game, something happened. He had a chance for still *another* goal. He had the puck and he could have shot. He could perhaps have become the only man in hockey history to have scored *51* goals in 50 games. What a record *that* would be!

He lined up to take the shot. Then he stopped.

His linemate, Bryan Trottier, was coming down the other side. He had an even better angle on the goal. He had a better shot. So Bossy flicked the puck over to "Trots," who scored.

That is the type of player Mike Bossy is.

The intensity of the game is shown in the faces of
Marcel Dionne (*in front*) and his New York Ranger
pursuer, Garry Howatt.

T W O

MARCEL DIONNE

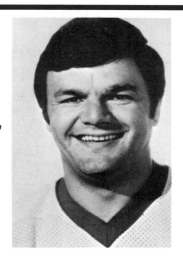

Marcel Dionne often visits his hometown of Drummondville, Quebec. He is welcomed as a local boy who made good because today Dionne is one of hockey's greatest stars. He gets along fine with the people in his hometown. They seem to love him and he loves them.

But once some of these same people were angry at the Dionne family. The local newspaper called Marcel a "traitor." The town's leaders threatened to take him to court.

Because he was a *bad* hockey player? No, because he was a *good* hockey player. One of the best in all of junior hockey in Canada. The people in the United States enjoy hockey. But maybe not yet as much as the people in Canada. In Canada, hockey is the most important sport of all.

As a teenaged player for the Drummondville Rangers, Dionne decided to join a rival team. He wanted to move from the Rangers to the St. Catharines Black Hawks. The new team was in Ontario, in a different junior league.

Dionne knew it was a tougher league. The players were better than the players in Drummondville. He felt that playing with his new team would make him a better player. His goal was to become a professional hockey player.

So he wanted to leave Drummondville. But the people in Drummondville didn't like that idea. They wanted him to stay on the home team.

That's when Dionne's relatives came up with a plan.

Dionne's uncles had always helped him in his career. As a young player, he remembers how they sat in the kitchen and talked about him. Sometimes they would be joined by Dionne's older brother, sisters, parents and grandparents. They all planned the career of *Le p'tit Marcel* (little Marcel).

Sometimes the relatives would take up a collection. They would buy a new stick or some other piece of equipment for Dionne. They knew that someday he would be a star player. But they knew he had to change teams. So they dreamed up this plan.

Dionne's parents pretended to separate. They did this because some people were saying they would sue Marcel if he left town. Mrs. Dionne moved to St. Catharines with Marcel, his brother and three sisters. When Marcel was settled in on his new team, the others moved back home. But the people in Drummondville stared at them and didn't like them. And they let the Dionnes know how they felt.

Hockey is *very* serious business in Canada.

Getting started in hockey is not easy, according to Dionne. It is a "long process."

"I started when I was five. Now kids are starting when they are *three*," Dionne said. "It is like little league baseball in the United States. But in Canada there is a draft of young players. Hockey players can come into the big league at eighteen or nineteen years old."

Dionne considers his move to St. Catharines as the turning point in his career. But not because of the hockey team he joined.

Instead, it was because of the *school* he attended. "I was lost and alone," he recalled. "I was French-Canadian and couldn't speak English at all. The school was basically English with only one-percent French.

"I became aware that it doesn't matter in what language you meet people. They are all the same people. I mastered two languages by learning English. It was a turning point for me. I can go anywhere in the world and understand because English is number one and French is not too far behind. This has helped me *tremendously.*"

There were two superstar players in youth hockey during Dionne's years in the junior league after he joined the Black Hawks. One was Marcel himself. The other was a skillful young player by the name of Guy Lafleur.

When the time came for player draft, pro teams fought for the services of these two. Finally, Dionne went to the Detroit Red Wings. Lafleur went to the Montreal Canadiens. Both players soon became stars in the National Hockey League.

Lafleur was happy. He remained with the Canadiens.

But Marcel Dionne was not happy. The fans in

Detroit thought he was stuck-up. They said he didn't work hard enough on the ice. They shouted out that he was poor on defense. No matter how hard Dionne tried, the fans weren't happy.

So Dionne asked to be traded to another team. That made things even worse in Detroit. The crowd began to boo him. In fact, to this day, the fans in Detroit boo when Dionne skates out on the ice of Olympia Stadium.

Hockey fans can be almost as tough as the players.

Finally Dionne was traded. He joined the Los Angeles Kings in 1975.

Los Angeles was a whole new world for Dionne. He liked the warm weather and the beaches. He liked the people.

They liked him, too. The moment he skated onto the ice of the Forum, they began to cheer. At last he had found a team that respected what he could do. Marcel Dionne soon became one of the most valuable players in hockey history.

In his first season with the Kings, he set new team records. He scored 40 goals and 54 assists. In his second season, 1976–77, he scored 53 goals and 69 assists. These were new team records, *and* new records for Dionne. That same year he was on the all-star team and won the Lady Byng Trophy. This award is given to the player who shows the most sportsmanship in the NHL. He had won the same trophy in Detroit in 1975, but the fans there didn't seem to care.

Dionne was injured during the 1977–78 season. He suffered a shoulder injury. But even then, he scored 36 goals and 43 assists.

His shoulder healed and he started scoring again. The next season he scored 59 goals for the Kings. And he helped on 71 of his teammates' goals. His total points for 1978–79 was 130. Dionne was getting better and better.

Streaking down the ice with his short, choppy moves, he became the dread of goalies. His wrist shot was more like an accurate lightning bolt than a hockey shot. Often the goalie wouldn't even see the puck before it was slamming into the back of the net. Around the league the crowds were always larger when Dionne was scheduled to play.

1979–80 was a hockey player's dream for Marcel Dionne. He was a scoring machine. Once again healthy and injury-free, he scored 53 goals and assisted on 84 others. His 137 points led the entire National Hockey League. For his skill on the ice, he was awarded a spot as center on the first-string all-star team. He won the Art Ross Trophy for being the league's leading scorer. He was selected Player of the Year by a poll of players in the *Sporting News*.

There was yet another trophy, a tall silver one. It is proudly displayed by Dionne. The Lester B. Pearson Memorial Award is given to the Most Valuable Player of the year. It is voted by all the other NHL players. Marcel Dionne won the award for the 1978–79 season and again for the 1979–80 season.

For years, Dionne has been compared with Guy Lafleur. Both players are stars. Crowds cheer them wherever they go (except for Dionne in Detroit). Each player is the star on his own team. Yet Guy Lafleur's face is unscarred.

The face of Marcel Dionne has more than seventy stitches from cutting injuries. His nose has been broken four times. He is constantly bumped and shoved by the enemy players.

Montreal, where Lafleur plays, probably has better defensive players. They seem to protect

A breakaway is one of the most exciting moments in hockey. ***Top:*** Marcel Dionne (*left*) grabs the puck from a defenseman. ***Bottom:*** Then he skates in alone on the goalie. ***Opposite:*** The hooking harassment and the fall are often a part of a breakaway.

their star better than the Los Angeles Kings protect Dionne. Dionne sometimes must fight off his attackers himself. Hockey experts have said that if Dionne played for Montreal, he would be even better than he is.

"If they would go by the rule book, my opponent would be in the penalty box all night," said Dionne. Then he sighs. "Oh well, maybe I'll get plastic surgery when it's over."

Meanwhile, a battered nose did once add to Dionne's goal scoring. The game was against the St. Louis Blues. One of the Kings' players, Rob Palmer, raised his stick high. His slap shot screamed toward the goalie of St. Louis, Mike Liut. Dionne was near the goal, struggling with a pack of players. The puck seemed to rise as it sped through the air. It slammed directly into Marcel's nose.

Then into the goal.

Even Dionne was amazed when the red light went on.

He was taken into the locker room for more stitches. "When you're hot," he mused, "you're *hot!*"

Marcel Dionne is short and stocky. Some of his

Kings teammates have nicknamed him Lou. That stands for comedian Lou Costello, also a rather pudgy man. Dionne doesn't mind. He often wears a gold belt buckle with LOU in 3-inch-high letters. It was given to him by one of his teammates.

Dionne's shoulders and arms are huge. He developed these muscles from carrying beer cases to the family store in Canada. The Dionne family ran a grocery called *Epicerie Dionne* when Dionne was a young player. In the summers, he worked on his uncle's farm in Canada. This made his legs solid and muscular.

One writer said, "If all the structures in Southern California had Dionne's center of gravity, earthquakes would be far less fearsome."

Marcel Dionne is built low, solid, muscular and tough. Yet on the ice he is quick as lightning. When he grabs the puck and skates for the goal, the crowd rises to its feet. He is very exciting to watch.

Dionne's teammates get ready. Dionne may shoot with a quick flip of his wrists. Or he may look one way and pass the puck another way to a teammate. The poor goalie must just wait and watch. He never knows what is going to happen.

More often than not the puck will slip into the net from a different direction than the one he expects!

Marcel Dionne lives in a fine home in Palos Verdes, California. It has a cloverleaf swimming pool and many bedrooms. Often new teammates stay there before they find a home. Many relatives visit Dionne from Canada. Dionne and his wife, Carol, and young son and daughter seem to enjoy visitors.

"I like people," said Dionne. "I believe in enjoying them."

Marcel Dionne can afford such a fine home. He can afford to entertain relatives and friends. In 1980 he signed the best contract of any hockey player up to that time. His team owner, Dr. Jerry Buss, was making sure that Dionne stayed in Los Angeles. Dionne's contract made him the highest-paid player in hockey. He is one of the highest-paid athletes in all of sports.

That seems to be just fine with Dionne. He has no intention of leaving Los Angeles anyhow. By now he owns land up and down California. He owns condominiums. He is wealthy and getting more wealthy all the time.

Behind the goal, Dionne shows the glee of every
hockey player after he scores.

Dionne's hobby is collecting baseball caps. He has more than fifty, and he is always looking for new ones. Dionne loves baseball almost as much as hockey. He is a fan of the Los Angeles Dodgers. Wherever the Kings go, he tries to see at least one baseball game.

Fans and players have given Dionne several nicknames. Gordie Howe, a famous hockey player, always calls him Little Beaver. Some players call him Fat Cat. Dionne doesn't mind. Most recently they have begun to call him Tattoo. Anybody who has seen the TV show "Fantasy Island" knows that Tattoo, like Dionne, is rather short.

Marcel Dionne is very important to the Los Angeles Kings. He has more goals and assists than anybody else on his team. His line in 1980–81 was called the Triple Crown line. He was in the center. On one wing was Charlie Simmer. On the other was Dave Taylor. The Triple Crown line scared more goals than any other line on any other team in hockey in that season.

But when Marcel Dionne is injured, the team begins to lose games. When he is well, they win far more often.

Marcel Dionne has never done what he most

wants to do in hockey. He has never played on a team that has won the Stanley Cup. The cup is the trophy for the best team in hockey. This is the team that beats all the other teams in a wild and exciting playoff series of games.

Guy Lafleur has won a Stanley Cup. More than once. So have many other players. Some of them are not nearly as good as Dionne. Winning the tall silver cup is Dionne's dream. He keeps hoping it might happen in Los Angeles. If the other players on the Kings play as well as he plays, the team can do it.

THREE

WAYNE GRETZKY

No player had ever scored six assists in one Stanley Cup playoff game. It would be a *fine* record to own. It could be very important to your career as a hockey player.

Wayne Gretzky of the Edmonton Oilers had already assisted on five goals in the 1981 game against Montreal. He would set a new all-time record with just one more assist.

Suddenly there was a flurry of players in front of the Montreal goal. The goalie grabbed for the puck. But it was too late. The puck was in the net.

The siren screamed and the red light flashed on. The crowd roared.

Then the announcement came booming down from the public address system. Wayne Gretzky, the youngest player on the ice, had just assisted on another goal. He had broken the long-standing record. He had *six* assists in one playoff game. Another roar came from the crowded grandstands.

"Wait a minute!" said Gretzky as he skated over to the referee. "I didn't even touch the puck. The assist is not mine." He refused to accept a record he really hadn't set.

A player like Wayne Gretzky is rare in sports. To Gretzky, it was far more important to win the game. The record was second. They did win the game. Gretzky helped on every goal.

In the 1980–81 season the Edmonton Oilers scored a total of 328 goals. Gretzky himself scored or assisted on 164 of them. That's one-half of all the goals of more than twenty players. Gretzky was brand-new in the NHL that year. It was only his second season and he was only twenty years old. Yet he broke every scoring record in the books with 109 assists and 55 goals. He became the highest-scoring player in hockey history for a single season. And that was *nothing* compared to what the amazing Gretzky did in his *third* season.

"A magician ... a magician," said Montreal

coach Claude Ruel. "Every night he thinks up new things to do."

Sports writer Gordon Edes described Gretzky in the *Los Angeles Times*. "He is a blue-and-orange flame, flickering all over the ice while trying to avoid being snuffed out by defensemen several inches and forty pounds bigger."

"People think I get out of the way of checks [body blocks] because I'm clever," says the slightly built Gretzky. "I get out of the way to save my *life*."

When the Oilers tested their players for upper body strength, Gretzky came in dead last. So he is very careful on the ice. But in the same test, *stamina* was judged. Although thin and quite harmless appearing, Gretzky did so well that the doctors thought their machine was broken.

Even as a child growing up in Canada, Wayne Gretzky was smaller than many other boys his age. But he and his two brothers were skating as soon as they could walk. The Gretzky boys' father saw to that. Most Canadian fathers are hockey fans like Walter Gretzky. He wanted his boys to have a chance in the big league, the National Hockey League.

He knew they would have to start early and work hard.

All but Wayne, that is. Everybody thought that Wayne was going to be too little to play professional hockey. Hockey players have to be big and strong. They have to be able to take a solid beating in every game. Hockey is a rough sport. Walter Gretzky recalls that Wayne was "so tiny he would have to take four strides to everyone else's one."

The other brothers might have a chance. But not Wayne. Still Wayne tried. Then he tried some more. All he could think about was his great idol, Gordie Howe. Howe is one of the greatest hockey players in history.

But it didn't come easy for Wayne Gretzky. He practiced very hard . . . for *years*. Every fall Walter Gretzky would set up a sprinkler in the Gretzky backyard in Brantford, Ontario. All night long the sprinkler would run. Night after night in the freezing Canadian winters. The entire backyard would become as smooth as glass with ice. It

Top: Gretzky (*far left*) tries to jam the puck under the goalie. *Bottom:* He then must face one of hockey's goal crease battles.

would become a do-it-yourself ice-skating rink. That's where a determined Wayne Gretzky practiced and practiced.

Here is his schedule during the winter as a six-year-old schoolboy. He would get home from school about 3:30 in the afternoon. On would go his skates.

Soon the other boys in the neighborhood would show up with their skates and equipment. They began a hockey game. Every day, day after day, the boys would play hockey on the Gretzky backyard rink. By 5:30 it would be time for dinner. The other boys would go home.

"After dinner I'd go out and skate some more," said Wayne Gretzky. "Except for Tuesday, Wednesday and Saturday. On those nights, there would be a hockey game on television at 8:00, so I'd go watch."

The only trouble was, he could only watch the first two periods on Tuesday and Wednesday. His dad would make him go to bed because of school the next day. During the week, Wayne hardly ever saw the third period of a hockey game.

Still, there were a few minutes between the end of the second period and bedtime. Can you guess what young Gretzky did then? He went back out and skated a while longer.

"Unlike many of the other kids," Wayne's father recalls, "Wayne never fooled around much in practice. He was always dead serious about it."

On some days, of course, Wayne would ease up just like any other young man. He just didn't feel like practicing.

So his father would say, "Someday when you're working a nine-to-six job, maybe you'll feel like it."

"His message got through," Wayne Gretzky recalled.

The long practice sessions continued. The young player put his heart into the game.

In Canada there is a series of leagues for hockey called the juniors. Young players work up to better and better competition according to their age and skill. The trouble was, Gretzky had become so good through practice, skill and raw talent, he was always "ahead of himself." When he was ten he was playing fifteen-year-old players. When he was fifteen, he was playing eighteen- and nineteen-year-olds.

Gretzky was only ten years old when television

found him. He was the subject of a long television interview. A few years later he was often seen in newspapers and magazines. People would stand in lines to watch him play. Why? Because he had scored 387 goals already. He had become a scoring machine. He was the best player in youth hockey.

In January, 1979, when he was nineteen, Gretzky was lined up on a World Hockey Association All-Star team. He was among the greatest players in the sport. On his left wing was Mark Howe, Gordie's son. And on his right wing? Playing on the same ice, on the very same team? It was Gordie Howe, himself. It was, according to Wayne Gretzky, the biggest thrill of his life.

Wayne Gretzky played for the Indianapolis Racers of the World Hockey Association. This was his first professional experience. But soon after he began, the league folded. So the owner of the Edmonton Oilers bought his contract.

Not many people know why Gretzky wears the number 99 on his uniform. That's how long his contract with the Oilers is for. Until 1999. The Oilers got him for their team. They want to make sure they *keep* him.

Even today, though he is a super-champion, Gretzky practices hard. He practices after the team has quit. He gets another player to stand in front of the goal. Then he gets behind the goal. He takes shot after shot out and around the net, trying to bounce the puck into the goal off the goalie's skates.

Does all this practice and skill help? By mid-March of the 1981–82 season, Wayne Gretzky had wiped out every goal-scoring record ever set in the NHL. He had become the most feared, respected shooter in the league.

Remember the struggle for Maurice Richard to reach 50 goals in 50 games? It was a long-standing record in the NHL. It took many years, but finally Mike Bossy came along and tied the record.

One year after Bossy tied Richard's record, Wayne Gretzky *shattered* it. He reached his fiftieth goal in only 39 games.

Before the end of the season, before the play-offs even started, he had scored 92 goals. Only Mike Bossy had come close to that. He had scored 85 goals, and his goals included the Stanley Cup playoff games.

It had become obvious that Gretzky was going

to score more than two hundred points in that single season. Nobody had ever come *close* to that. Finally, he did reach and exceed this amazing total with a final count of 212 points.

To show their appreciation of this hockey whiz, the Edmonton Oilers gave him a new contract. Oh, it still runs until 1999. But his new contract raises his pay from "only" $150,000 per year (plus a couple of hundred thousand in endorsements) to over *one million dollars per year.*

That is nearly a *20-million-dollar* contract, the highest of any hockey star in history. And perhaps the highest for any sports figure in all of history.

Although Gretzky has grown, by NHL standards he is still small. He is a slim, 5-feet 11-inch, 165-pound player. But he is a top scorer in all of hockey in spite of having to fight off two or three tough defensive players *all the time.*

Defensemen are not gentle with him, not in the NHL. They slam him into the side boards and end boards. They lift his stick off the puck. They harass him. If the referee isn't watching, they slash and cross-check him. They try anything to keep him off the puck.

Gretzky smiles. "You know the NHL. They

Gretzky faces off against Dan Bonar at the Forum
in Los Angeles.

clutch and grab and some teams try to play dirty.
But it's a challenge and it keeps you going. I love
playing the game. It's no different than little kids
who go out and play for the fun of it. We're just
big kids playing a game. I love playing and I enjoy
the thrill of winning.''

Gretzky is modest. He claims that he cannot
skate all that well. Not as well as several other
players, he says. His hardest shot, he insists,

"wouldn't break a pane of glass." He is always giving credit for his own great success to the other two players on his line.

Yet Wayne Gretzky has uncanny instincts. He can see the entire rink in an instant. He seems to be able to guess where everybody will be in two or three more seconds. He shoots the puck through the legs of several players toward a spot on the ice where nobody is skating. By the time the puck gets there, one of Gretzky's teammates is waiting.

One place the enemy doesn't want Gretzky is behind the goal. From here he can slip the puck to any one of several players.

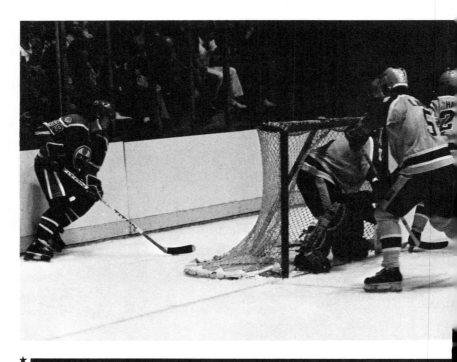

Instantly, there is a speeding slap shot. More often than not, the enemy goalie is caught by surprise. The Edmonton Oilers have another goal, and Wayne Gretzky has another assist.

Young Wayne Gretzky, like Mike Bossy, is a ghost on the ice. He suddenly appears where the enemy least wants him to be. In spite of their guarding, he streaks off with the puck. One player said, "When he has the puck, anybody else on the team can get a shot."

Gretzky skims behind the enemy goal and stops in a spray of ice. His teammates come sweeping in. They slide down the slot, toward the goalie. Meanwhile, Gretzky fights off his guards.

The poor goalie doesn't know what to do. Or where to run. He pivots back and forth, trying to watch Gretzky and the oncoming players. The puck will zip out to one player. Or another. Or another. Nobody knows where it will go, but the pass will be exactly on the stick. With a quick flip of the wrists, the player will put the puck in the goal.

It is *beautiful* hockey to watch.

By the end of the 1981–82 season, Wayne Gretzky had broken many records. In only his

The puck is coming in from a defenseman. Gretzky (*center*) will instantly flick it at the goal.

third year of pro hockey, he set the record for the quickest 50 goals ever scored. He had the most goals in a single season of any player, ever. He had the most goals in a single season, including playoffs, of any player ever. He had the most assists of any player ever. He had the most total points of any player in history. He had the most hat tricks (three goals in a single game) of any player in history. He had the highest point average per game of any player in the NHL, ever.

In Canada and in hockey around the world Gretzky has already picked up a nickname. He is called Gretzky the Great.

But Wayne Gretzky is only beginning his career. His great skill will excite hockey fans for many years to come.

With wry humor, another hockey star groans, "It's frightening to think how good he will be when he grows up."

FOUR

DENIS POTVIN

"I like hitting and I like to play *mean!*" says Denis Potvin. Potvin is a defenseman for the Stanley Cup champion New York Islanders. He is also the team's captain.

More than one team in the NHL plays according to a simple rule. That rule is, "get to the puck first and arrive in poor humor."

The game is especially tough for defensemen. They guard their own goal. They help their goalie as the enemy forwards rush toward them. They try to get the puck and feed it off to one of their own forwards.

They can do this by stealing the puck from the stick of the enemy forward. They can be tricky. Or they can just slam into the oncoming forward with their hip or shoulder. This knocks him down.

Then they take the puck and pass it to their own forward. Potvin is *very* good at this.

Meanwhile, defensemen must block shots at their own goal. Way out on the ice, the enemy forwards are fighting to get control of the puck. Then one enemy player skids to a stop. His stick rises high in the air. It blurs down to the puck.

It is a slap shot!

The puck screams across the ice at over one hundred miles per hour. You are your team's defenseman and it is heading toward the goal, *your* goal. What do you do? Most of the really good defensemen in the NHL try to block the shot with their stick. Or their leg. Or their arm. But if it is too late for any of that, they do something else. They simply drop to the ice in front of the puck. They block the shot with their *body*.

Yes, the puck can injure them. In spite of the padding they wear. The puck is a hard, frozen chunk of rubber coming like a bullet. That's why the bodies of defensemen are covered with bruises. But *anything* is better than letting the enemy get a goal.

Denis Potvin is considered by most experts to be the best all-around defenseman in the NHL.

He is also considered by Denis Potvin to be the best defenseman in the NHL. Potvin is proud and very sure of himself. He was raised on hockey in Canada. His brothers played hockey before him. His brother Jean plays hockey for the same New York Islanders.

Denis Potvin is famous for another hockey move as well as for slamming into forwards. He grabs the puck from the enemy and then rushes up the ice by himself. He is an *offensive*-defenseman. He can score as well as prevent the enemy from scoring.

When Denis Potvin was growing up, his father was like many other Canadian fathers. He wanted to see his sons play professional hockey. In fact, he himself had wanted to play hockey in the pros. Armand Potvin had been a star in Canadian junior hockey. He had been invited to play for the Detroit Red Wings. But a serious injury had ended his playing career.

So Armand Potvin built a rink in his backyard for his sons, Jean, Bob and Denis. By the time Denis was three years old, he was skating with his older brothers. He wore the skates his father had worn as a child.

His older brothers took care of young Denis. And the younger brother was welcome at the older boys' games. This may not be true with many games between brothers, but it was with the Potvin brothers.

The reason was that Denis Potvin was *good* at hockey. This was very plain early in his career.

Eventually, Denis Potvin became one of the finest young hockey players in the junior leagues in Canada. But Jean got to the New York Islanders first. Some experts insist that Jean was hired by the team so that it would be easier to get Denis when the time came. The two brothers (the third went into another business) are very close. They think that's how it should be with brothers.

So Jean was hired by the Islanders. Then along came Denis. He was a first-round draft pick. Everybody expected him to do very well in the NHL.

He didn't disappoint them. In his first year, 1974, he was chosen the winner of the Rookie of the Year Award. He was the best first-year player in the whole NHL.

In 1976, Denis Potvin was awarded the James

Norris Memorial Trophy for the first time. This trophy is given to the best defenseman in the entire league. He won it again in 1978. That same year he scored 30 goals and had 70 assists. This made him the only defenseman since Bobby Orr to score 100 points in a single season.

Potvin is hard and tough. Yet he has a smooth, graceful way of skating. He can pick up a puck and skate in and around enemy players all the way to the goal. Not many defensemen can do this. Nor are very many defensemen known to be good scorers, as Potvin is. He is one of the highest-scoring defensemen in the big league.

Hockey players play under conditions of physical pain that would stop most athletes. Often they get cut in a game. They skate to the bench and the trainer sews them up. Then they skate back into the game. Generally they turn down any pain-killing medicine because it would hurt their game.

Denis Potvin played most of the 1973–74 season with a broken foot. It was his first year and he *had* to look good. So he played in intense pain most of the time.

When Potvin is not working, he spends his off-

Opposite: Denis Potvin crashes into the goal, falls to the ice, and (*above*) rolls over in pain.

duty time in New York City visiting museums and art galleries. He has a deep love for art and music. At home, he has a fine music collection.

For a time, his love of the arts hurt him with some of his teammates. They didn't understand somebody who liked to listen to music. Or to look at pictures in a museum. They began to think that he was stuck-up. Maybe he didn't think they had any culture, or so they thought. Potvin did seem to be a loner. He enjoyed the company of his brother. But he didn't seem to go out of his way to make friends with his teammates.

"I am very sensitive," Potvin told the *New York Times,* "though at times I wish I weren't because things would be easier. I have incredible highs and incredible lows. It's very difficult for me to stay in the middle."

Even today, Potvin claims to "hate crowds." He enjoys blending in with the crowds on the streets of New York City. He doesn't seem to want to be noticed. "The best times of my life have been spent fishing on some isolated lake," he insists.

After a game, Potvin must meet the press. He is a sports star and they have questions to ask. Generally he is cordial and even witty. But then he soon wants to leave. He wants to go outside and blend in with the people.

But to succeed *during* a hockey game, there are certain things that every hockey defenseman should have. Not many have all of these things. Potvin has.

A defenseman must be very physical. Denis

Potvin is big, at six feet and over two hundred pounds. He is a crippling hitter. When you are in the corner or at the blue line and hit by him, you go down. Hitting is legal in the NHL. It is called checking and must be done in a certain way to prevent injury. It is just a part of ice hockey.

Defensemen must have stamina. Potvin is known to be able to play at his peak through most of the game. He can be sent in for shifts on the ice more often than most other defensemen. He doesn't seem to need the brief rest periods between shifts on the ice.

The best defenseman must be able to pass the puck up the ice with pinpoint accuracy. Denis Potvin has always been able to pass right on the stick of his forwards. And he does it with a quick flip of his wrists that is beautiful to see.

Potvin certainly has everything a defenseman needs. And his playing helped his team win the Stanley Cup.

In 1980, the New York Islanders won the Stanley Cup for the first time in their history. They had only been a team in the NHL since 1972. That was the year several new teams were formed. Only the Philadelphia Flyers won the famous cup sooner after their creation.

Being in the middle of things all the time, as Potvin often is, can be costly. His body has suffered. Plagued by injuries, he was almost sidelined during the 1981–82 season and his points totals dropped. But he continued to fight back, regaining his confidence.

Potvin has other interests outside hockey, music, and art. He has become interested in Transcendental Meditation. "I get enjoyment from it as well as a lot out of it," he told hockey writer Bill Libby. "All I do is take twenty minutes early in the day to be by myself and to meditate. It's a system for getting off and clearing your mind.

"It may sound like a freaky thing, but I have found it fascinating, personally. I didn't have to shave my head and stand on it. I just had to relax and give it a chance to work for me. It has worked for me," he told Libby.

Many give Potvin direct credit for the fact that the Islanders are the champions. But not exactly for his leadership. Not at first, anyhow.

Potvin was not the best-liked man on the team

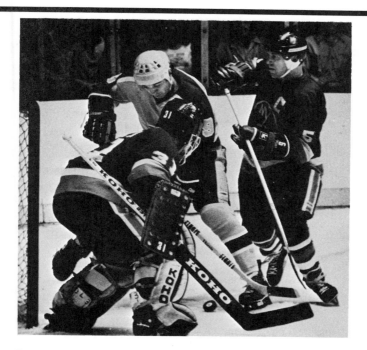

Potvin (*right*) has allowed an enemy forward to get between him and his goalie. He'll take him out with a body check.

in the earlier days. He was different. He liked things the other players weren't interested in. Though he was winning hockey awards from the NHL, his teammates didn't quite know how to take him. And they disliked something he had written in a newspaper after the Canada Cup games in 1975.

Potvin played with the best players in hockey in those games. After the games, he wrote a story for a Canadian newspaper. In the story, he praised the great Bobby Orr. He said it was nice that Orr had won the Most Valuable Player award for the games. The Canadian team had beaten the Soviet Union team with the help of both Orr and Potvin.

Then Potvin went on to write that he had played even better than Orr. He, Potvin, should have been considered more strongly for the award.

His teammates were angry with him. Orr was one of the greatest players in hockey history. To say anything against Bobby Orr seemed to them to be speaking against hockey itself.

Then came the turning point for Potvin and the Islanders. He called a meeting with his teammates. He said he was wrong for writing what he wrote.

After that the team began playing as a unit. They became the champions. Denis Potvin became their captain.

It has been that way since. Potvin is a smart, smooth athlete. But he hits *hard*. Famous coach Scotty Bowman said, "He doesn't just hit people. He *hurts* them. He lays on the wood when he's throwing a body check. He leaves his mark."

"I just play best when I play tough hockey," Potvin told *Hockey Today*. "I play aggressively and use my bulk to get the puck. If that brings on a reputation as being mean, well, I can't change that."

Denis Potvin became the number one defenseman in the entire NHL. He wears the C of the captain on his jersey. Under his guidance, the Islanders won the Stanley Cup again in 1981. They were the top team in hockey for the second year in a row. Potvin had set a new NHL record for most points (25) by a defenseman in a playoff series.

Still Potvin didn't stop. He guided his team to yet another Stanley Cup in 1982. The New York Islanders became one of the few teams ever to win the great silver cup three times in a row.

With a proud smile on his face, Potvin held the huge cup high over his head. He skated around the ice. The crowd was roaring their pleasure. The cup is huge. It appears quite heavy. Only the winners get to carry it around the rink.

One reporter shouted at Potvin. "How much does it weigh?" Potvin grinned. "That cup doesn't weigh an *ounce* when you're carrying it around."

FIVE

JIM CRAIG

He *is* a super-champion. But not in the National Hockey League. Not yet. It could even be said about him that he is a failure in the NHL. By 1981, he had been bumped off the end of the Boston Bruins' bench.

He had been ordered to the minors. Sent down. Replaced.

But if you had to bet on somebody to become an NHL super-champion, keep him in mind.

Meanwhile, on another team he was one of the most famous champions of all. His name is Jim Craig. His greatest fame came at Lake Placid, New York. No matter how great he becomes in the NHL, he might never top Lake Placid.

Few had heard of Jim Craig before the 1980 Olympics at Lake Placid. Even after the Games started, few paid much attention. The United States team was a collection of young American players from colleges and amateur teams. They were good. You must be good to be on an Olympic team.

But nobody really expected them to be much better than fifth or sixth in the world. Many countries support their Olympic team better than the United States supports its team. The Russian team, for example, had played together for a long time. They were a *team* in the best sense of the word.

Everybody said that the Russians would win the Olympics in ice hockey. There seemed to be little question about that. They had won the last three Olympics.

But then as the long round of hockey games went on, people began to pay more attention. The U.S. team had played the Swedish team to a tie in the first round. Then they *beat* the tough Czechoslovakian team. These were *good* hockey teams. Suddenly, Americans began to watch their team more closely. It was possible, barely possible, that the young team could go all the way to one of the final games.

Of course, everyone said they could not beat the Russians. The Russians were also winning in their round of games, as expected. But the U.S. team was doing better than most people had dared hope.

In the next series of games, the U.S. team beat Norway. Then it beat Romania. The whole United States was paying attention by then. These were *powerful* hockey teams.

The U.S. team had come together as a unit. The members were playing as a team. They had spirit. They believed they could win. They even thought they could go all the way to winning the gold medal.

Next they defeated the strong West Germany hockey team. Suddenly they were in the semifinal round of the Games.

Who was the other team in the semifinal round?

The Russians!

The winner would go on to play one final game against a team from Finland that was weaker than the Russian team.

It was a wild and exciting semifinal round. By then millions of people were watching this young

American team on television. You didn't have to be a hockey fan to be a viewer. Everybody, it seemed, was watching and talking about the team. They had captured the attention of the United States.

But could they really beat the Russians? They could, and *did*—4-3. It was a stunning victory for the United States team.

Finally they beat Finland 4-2, and that was it. The "miracle" was complete. The nation was proud and happy. The exciting young U.S. team had won the hockey gold medal. It had seemed impossible, but the team had done it.

Standing on the ice, an American flag draped around his shoulders, was the young goalie of the U.S. team. He had played the entire series. All the players had played very well. But the goalie had played best of all. With his leaping, stabbing, sprawling saves, he had won the games. As the whole country cheered, Jim Craig looked up into the stands for his father. He wanted to share the big moment with him.

Jim Craig became famous just that quickly. After the Olympics, the other passengers would stand and applaud when he got on an airplane.

He was on talk shows. He endorsed products. He made speeches.

Craig went to Indianapolis to see the great Indy 500 auto race. The race organizers put him in the celebrity parade of cars that haul famous people around the track before the race begins. Every year, movie stars and famous politicians ride in open convertibles in the parade. Sports heroes and former race drivers ride too. Everybody is somebody. The crowd, more than 350,000, roar their approval.

When the car with Jim Craig rolled by, they roared louder and louder. The din was deafening. Many people were weeping from the great emotion of the moment.

Craig smiled shyly and waved, still uncertain about his newfound fame.

To no one's surprise, the National Hockey League wanted Jim Craig. They wanted him as a goalie in the pro ranks. Not only was Craig a fine goalie. He would also bring attention to whatever team he was on.

Craig wanted to be a goalie in the NHL. In fact, being an NHL goalie had been his dream for a long time.

But playing in a hockey goal is one of the most stressful positions in all of sports. Most goalies are covered with scars. Most have lost teeth to the game. Many have ulcers due to the great pressure of their position. Goalies are the last line of defense for their team. In hockey, one goal is often the difference between victory and defeat. When all else fails, the goalie must stop the puck.

One goalie got sick during each game he played in the NHL. The trainers kept a bucket handy for him. But he was a fine goalie otherwise. Another goalie had a terrible home life. He finally got a divorce because he couldn't get along with his wife. Still another jumped and became upset when he would hear sharp sounds, or see a red light. A red light, as every fan knows, means a goal has been scored.

A forward may play poorly for most of the game, then score in the last couple of minutes and win the game. He is a hero. A goalie may play very well for most of the game, then allow one easy goal in the last minute and lose it. He is a *goat*.

Goalies play with a very small margin for error. They cannot misjudge the angles. They cannot permit many rebounds.

But a goalie is what Jim Craig wanted to be. This is what the NHL wanted him to be. Even before the Olympic Games, he had been drafted by the Atlanta Flames, so now the Flames called him up.

The Flames had not been doing well. They were in danger of leaving Atlanta. They had only a few thousand fans at each game. Often less than that. They were losing money, a lot of money.

Jim Craig donned the red uniform of the Flames and instantly he was a hero once again. In his very first game, the arena was sold out. The crowd thundered their approval of the young American hero. He played very well and the Flames won the game.

But Jim Craig was finding fame difficult to handle. He began to feel that people expected too much from him. He had to be here, and there, and somewhere else, all at the same time. He couldn't go on the street without being recognized. It was exhausting.

The Flames were having trouble. So was Jim Craig. Hockey had made him famous and now hockey was beginning to suffer because of his fame. Craig was from a middle-class family in

Massachusetts. His mother and father had raised him and six other brothers and sisters. He was a quiet person from a modest background.

And suddenly he was dining with the President because he was an Olympic hero. He was being mobbed by people. He had an agent. He was making a lot of money.

But his game was suffering. He was under such pressure that he just wasn't playing well.

Then the Atlanta Flames folded. The team was sold to Calgary, in Canada.

For Jim Craig, it could have been the worst thing in the world. But instead, he was sent to Boston to play for the famous Bruins. It was more than he could have hoped for. Boston was almost his hometown. The Bruins had always been his favorite hockey team. The Boston coach, Gerry Cheevers, was a former goalie. He was also Craig's idol when Craig was in college.

Jim Craig was happy. He squared his shoulders and decided to handle things as he handled hockey games. He would not allow the fame from the Olympics to ruin his life. He wanted to become a solid part of the Bruins team. As its goalie,

Left: Craig has a word with referee Ron Wicks, but you can't see his lips moving.

Below: Coiled and ready, Craig watches the puck as the enemy moves in.

he would be in a high-pressure spot, but he would handle the pressure.

Craig had become a goalie almost by chance. The youth league in Massachusetts where he played provided equipment only to the goalie. Since Craig's father had a modest income, not having to pay for equipment was a lucky break.

During his years at Boston University, Craig grew to love hockey. He knew he wanted to make hockey his career. And he was a good goalie. Boston University became the champion of the league with Craig in the goal.

During those college years, he watched the great Bruins. He watched his idol, Cheevers, in the Bruins' goal. He wanted to be like Cheevers. Many NHL goalies decorate their masks with bright colors and symbols. Cheevers had his mask decorated with marks like stitched-up scars. Those were the scars he would have had, he explained, if he had not been wearing the mask. Each time a puck slammed into his mask, he would add a new scar mark.

Cheevers had been an interesting, popular goalie on a top team.

Now Jim Craig would be on the Bruin team.

True, he would be a back-up goalie behind the famous Rogie Vachon. But he would be playing in Bruins' games. The demanding Boston fans would be watching him.

But as soon as he began to play, he had new pressures. Every time he skated out onto the ice in Boston, great cheers rolled down from the stands. The tough Boston fans loved him because of the Olympics. They cheered him even before he played in a game. They expected him to perform the same miracles he had performed at Lake Placid, against the Russians.

Craig put more and more pressure on himself. He hated to lose. He didn't want to disappoint the fans. They had faith in him. The pressure became so great that gradually he became ill. Still he kept trying.

Nobody wins every game. Pro athletes are able to put losses behind them. Otherwise, each loss will affect the next game.

Finally, the Boston managers decided to send Craig down to a minor league team. They wanted to put him where he could play without so much pressure. They thought it would be good for Jim Craig. He could get back his game slowly there.

Craig had trouble in the NHL. Here, Charlie
Simmer scores against him.

But Craig didn't agree. He refused to be sent to
the minor league. He insisted on another chance.
Otherwise, he said he might not play again at all,
for any team.

From a national hero, Jim Craig had slipped to
a third-string goalie on a team that didn't really
want him. He had tried so hard to please everybody that he didn't seem to be able to please anybody. The harder he worked, the more goals the
enemy player seemed to score against him.

The Boston team understood that Craig did not

want to go down to the minors. They always wanted him to succeed. So the management gave him some time off to collect himself.

Even the Boston fans agreed. They expect a lot from their players. But they wanted Craig to succeed, so they waited.

Jim Craig began to work on his goalkeeping. He decided to cut back on his outside activities and concentrate on hockey. He worked hard on his game. He stayed home and practiced instead of flying around the country making speeches.

"In 2½ years, I had only 12 days off," said Craig. "When I look back on last year, I don't know how I got through it. I really don't. There are some things about it I don't even remember.

"I'm going to give everything I have to be the best player I can possibly be."

Craig was still in the Bruins' organization going into the 1981–82 season, but on a minor league team.

There is probably not one single hockey fan who hopes that he does not succeed. Even in the enemy rinks, Jim Craig is cheered. Most fans are hoping that Jim Craig makes good wherever he plays.

Lafleur can shoot while skating at high speed across the slot. He often scores.

SIX

GUY LAFLEUR

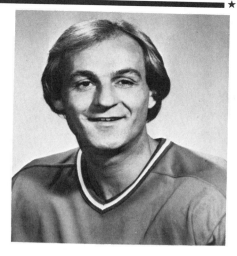

"On the ice, you see him here one second and the next second he's over there," said one famous hockey player.

The player was talking about Guy Lafleur. Every hockey fan knows the name is pronounced Ghee Lah-floor. If you are new to the game, you will soon hear the name spoken. Hockey is seldom discussed without a mention of him.

Lafleur is one of the greatest players in hockey today. And, according to many experts, in *history*.

As a youngster, Guy Lafleur loved to play hockey more than anything else. He practiced in the summer on roller skates. He would weave through his friends pushing a tennis ball with a stick. He would weave right then cut left. He would dodge about, pushing the tennis ball this way and that.

Again and again Lafleur would go through the whole crowd of his friends. They would try to get the ball away from him. But he would usually control it.

Lafleur would do the same thing in the winter, on ice. He would practice for hours. He loved the game.

In his mind Lafleur imagined that he was the great Jean Beliveau. Beliveau was a star player on the Montreal Canadiens. The Canadiens were one of the greatest teams in hockey history. Beliveau used skating skill rather than brute strength to get the puck in the goal.

He would use his stick like a magic wand instead of a club. Behind him he would leave a path of dazed defenders wondering how he got through.

Beliveau used to do it. So Lafleur practiced and practiced. Today he does it even better than Beliveau did.

Guy Lafleur is six feet tall and a rather thin 175 pounds. He has never had the bulk of many famous players. He was even thinner as a youth.

But still he dreamed of playing on the Canadiens.

The young Lafleur and his friends had a neighborhood team. It was a ragtag team with hand-me-down equipment. Among the equipment was a jersey from the Montreal Canadiens. The colors and emblem are famous in Canada and among American hockey fans. Every member of Lafleur's young team wanted to wear the "bleu, blanc, rouge" (blue, white, red) jersey. They would fight each other for the honor.

Little did the team know then that one of their members would one day wear the colors of the *real* Canadiens. Guy Lafleur did.

As a junior hockey player, Lafleur was a standout. He scored 130 goals for the Quebec Ramparts in the Quebec Junior League. This was in his final year as a junior. His total was up from 103 goals the year before. So he was expected to be a high-scoring player in the pros.

Lafleur was so good that he became the number one draft choice in the 1971 hockey draft. He was the number one player picked in the entire draft. Since the Montreal Canadiens were first to pick that year, he was also their number one draft choice.

So he was a Montreal Canadien, something he had long dreamed of being. But Guy Lafleur had a very shaky beginning as one of "The Habs," a nickname for the Canadiens.

In his first year with the mighty team, he scored only 29 goals. The NHL was quite differ-

Lafleur faces off while super-goalie Rogie Vachon, then with the Los Angeles Kings, waits.

ent from the juniors. But could it be *that* different? What was wrong? Was junior champion Lafleur only a flash in the pan? Lafleur fought back, trying his best to score. In his second year with the Canadiens, he dropped to a total of 28 goals.

For many hockey players, these numbers wouldn't be that bad. For the number one draft choice, they were terrible. It began to appear that Lafleur just couldn't make it with the Canadiens.

But the Montreal Canadiens didn't give up on Guy Lafleur. Players are brought along slowly and carefully on the Canadiens' team. The team doesn't thrust a new young player into a win-or-lose gamble. They work with their young players. They saw the great skill of the young French-Canadian. They kept him in the lineup. In his third year, he scored only 21 goals.

Lafleur felt he had hit bottom. His skill was evident, but he was not scoring well. "When I broke into the league, everybody expected me to score 50 goals," he later recalled. "I was frustrated because I didn't think I was getting enough ice time. I wanted to score 50 goals, too."

Off the ice, Lafleur had other problems. He was shy. He was a quiet young man who preferred home and family to running around with his teammates. He rarely spoke about anything. He was French-speaking in an English-speaking world. Also, he feared flying. Hockey teams must fly away to many games.

As with many people who succeed, Lafleur helped himself. What did he do about his fear of flying? He took flying lessons and learned to fly himself. He didn't speak English, so he moved to a Montreal suburb where only English was spoken. He forced himself to learn. Today, he speaks both French and English very well.

Back on the ice, he kept practicing and practicing his hockey. The turnaround for Guy Lafleur came in the 1974–75 hockey season. It was like the old days in the junior league. With great skill and polish he began to score goals. Before long he was the most feared player in the league. Not because he would play hard and tough, but because he was so good at scoring.

That year, Lafleur scored 53 goals. He had 66 assists. He won a position on the first team of the NHL All-Star team.

He won the same position among the best players in hockey for the next six years. He also be-

came the first NHL player ever to score 50 goals
or more in six seasons in a row.

Lafleur won the Art Ross Trophy as the
league's leading scorer in 1975–76, 1976–77 and
1977–78. He was awarded the Hart Memorial Trophy as the Most Valuable Player in both 1976–77
and 1977–78. Lafleur won the Conn Smythe Trophy as the Most Valuable Player in the Stanley
Cup playoffs in 1976–77.

Guy Lafleur is a celebrity in Canada. And in
American cities where hockey is a major sport. He
cannot go into a restaurant or store without being
mobbed by fans asking for his autograph. He
enjoys dressing like a champion. "He even wears
freshly pressed jeans to wash the car," says his
wife, Lise.

The Montreal Canadiens are the most noted
team in hockey. They have won the Stanley Cup
more than any other team. All of the players are
good. But when the team comes to town many
fans simply say "The Flower" (Lafleur) is in
town.

To see Guy Lafleur in one of his great streaks
down the ice is to see pure hockey at its finest.
With his long brown hair streaming out behind,

Above: Lafleur (*left*) battles with Butch Goring for control of the puck. His teammates wait for a pass.

Right: The man many say is the greatest player in hockey history waits in a corner for the puck.

he crosses the red line. Moving his stick side to side, he controls the puck. His eyes seem to take in the entire half of the ice. He seems to know where everybody is at every moment. And where they will be the next moment.

Here, for example, is a typical Guy Lafleur play. Lafleur's linemates are covered. So he flips the puck in a quick shot at the goalie. As the goalie is moving to block the puck, Lafleur is moving to where the rebound will be. The puck bounces from the goalie's pads and lands where Lafleur is waiting. He scoops it up, whirls around, and looks for another forward. They are still covered.

So he skates across the slot and fires a back-hand shot. It rings loudly off the metal goal post. The relieved goalie watches it skitter into the corner of the rink.

Without stopping, Lafleur swoops down on the puck. He slips it away from the nearest defense-man, spins around behind the net and tries to jam it in from the opposite side. The goalie is still expecting it from the other side, so he sprawls across the goal mouth.

Whether the puck goes in or not, Lafleur has created *three* scoring chances where none existed before. That is how he plays hockey. He never stops while he is on the ice. He has a smooth, flowing skating style and perfect puck control. He can be where you least expect him, and shoot when you least expect a shot.

When Lafleur gets the puck, no wonder the crowd rises to its feet to watch. Fans cheer when he starts his rush down the ice.

"He can beat you one-on-one almost anytime he wants," says one of the NHL's best defensemen, Brad Park. "All you can do is stand your ground and make him pass the puck off to someone else. Then you try to keep him from getting into the clear for a return pass. Lafleur is dangerous even when he doesn't have the puck," Park told Frank Orr of the *Toronto Star*.

In 1981–82, Lafleur was in his tenth season with the Canadiens. He had always wanted to play for them. He has never had any desire to leave them. The fans of the Canadiens hope he never leaves.

But despite his outstanding record, the 1981–82 season was a critical time for the great Lafleur. His position as the game's greatest living player was being challenged by other players.

Young Wayne Gretzky was coming on strong. The Los Angeles Kings' Marcel Dionne was being called the greatest by more experts than ever before.

The Canadiens were no longer the Stanley Cup champions. For two years in a row, the New York Islanders had won the cup. Mike Bossy had become a great scorer.

Lafleur himself had suffered serious knee injuries the previous season. His back had been giving him problems. He was unable to play in the Stanley Cup series in 1980–81. That was the season his team was eliminated in the first round.

Fans, hockey players and hockey experts still admire Lafleur tremendously. They watch him and note the beating he takes. "The amount of abuse Guy takes is unbelievable," says his teammate Larry Robinson. "He is constantly being hammered and fouled but he never allows it to bother him, never tries to retaliate and just keeps on going. It's as if he's saying 'you want to foul me, well, that's your problem, not mine.'"

They admire his grace and skill. Hockey writer Bill Libby described Guy Lafleur this way. "Lafleur typifies what is best about the sport. He is an artist on skates, creating scoring plays the way a painter puts a vivid scene on canvas with a brush."

All hockey fans hope that Guy Lafleur remains a super-champion in the NHL for years to come.

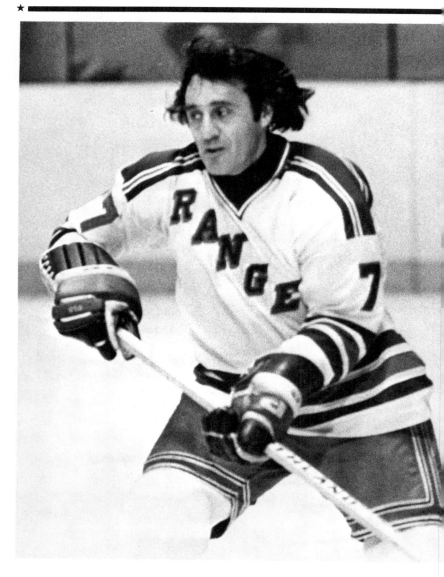

Esposito watches the puck like a hawk as he roars in on the poor goalie.

SEVEN

PHIL ESPOSITO

The slot is the area in front of the goal. The goalie doesn't want anybody in the slot. Watch any hockey game. You'll see defensemen trying to shove enemy players out of the slot.

Phil Esposito used to *plant* himself in the slot. He would skate to that area and *stay* there. He would suffer slashing and cross-checking and even fists from the defensemen. He wouldn't move.

Sooner or later, a loose puck would skim by. It would belong to nobody. It would be just moving around among the players.

Instantly, "Espo" would be on it. Like a spider on a fly, he would grab it with his stick. Then, with a flick of his wrists, he would flip it toward the goal.

The goalie could only flop to the ice to try to stop the puck. Sometimes he would stop it. But often he would not. Phil Esposito would have still another "garbage" goal.

A garbage goal in hockey is a goal scored from a random pass. A shot that wasn't planned. A shot off a rebound. The puck is merely stuffed into the net because it was there.

During his great NHL career Phil Esposito got more of these goals than anybody else. For 17 seasons, he was the "garbage goal man" of the NHL and one of the leading scorers.

This great player, who retired in 1980, was not always a super-champion in hockey.

Phil Esposito was a "hockey bum" in Canada. That's what Canadians called boys who dropped out of school to play hockey. The Canadian hockey system caused many boys to drop out of school. Later, most of them were very sorry.

Young boys would leave home to play hockey in the junior divisions. Sometimes they would be only fourteen years old. They were supposed to continue school in their new town. But often they would move from town to town as they were traded about. Few of them chose to continue

Espo was superb at scooping up loose pucks and flipping them into the goal.

studying. They wanted to play hockey. So they would drop out of school. They would become a hockey bum.

Phil Esposito did this. He dropped out of school after failing one year. He was put back into the grade of his younger brother, Tony. Finally he just dropped out. But he was sorry later.

Phil just loved playing hockey too much. All he wanted to do was play the game. He was born February 20, 1942, and for as long as he could remember he wanted to be a hockey player.

"When I grow up, I'm going to be a professional player," Esposito would say. His brother wanted to be a hockey player too. But he wanted to go to school, first.

When the two boys would play together, Phil would be the center. Tony wasn't as good a shot. So he would play goalie.

Most hockey fans know that Tony Esposito was a star goalie for many years on the Chicago Black Hawks' team. He was one of the best goalies of all. But it was older brother Phil who became a super-champion.

Even in the early days, Phil Esposito was good. But he was big and a little clumsy. When he finally got on the junior team he wanted, he had an accident. It sounds a little funny now. But it wasn't funny then.

Esposito's team, the St. Catherine's A team, was battling in the playoffs. The team was a farm team for the Chicago Black Hawks. The game was very important for St. Catherine's. If they could win, some of the players might move up to the major leagues. It was their big chance.

But then Phil, one of the star scorers, was sent to the penalty box. This wasn't too unusual. But what happened next *was* unusual. Especially since the team needed him very much.

Espo fell out of the penalty box. He just tripped and fell on the edge of the door. He tried to brace himself with his arm. His wrist snapped. It was *broken!*

Many people laughed when the big kid fell out of the box. But it wasn't funny to Phil, or to the team. He was out of the game and they lost the playoffs. Phil Esposito also lost his chance to be the top scorer in the whole league because of his broken wrist. He was nineteen years old. Time, he thought, was passing him by.

What did Espo do? He was desperate. He needed to be seen by the big league scouts from the Black Hawks. But the doctors told him if he played he could ruin his wrist for *life.*

Meanwhile, he had been sent down to a lesser team. So Phil decided to file down his cast. He cut it down so it would fit inside a hockey glove. Then he told his new coach he was all healed. The coach believed him and allowed him to play.

Imagine the pain! Imagine the chance he was taking on ruining his whole hockey career. But he *had* to play.

The scouts did see him. They offered him a contract to play for the Black Hawks' system. Today, players are getting almost a million dollars every year to play hockey in the big leagues. They offered Phil Esposito just under four thousand dollars. This wasn't very much money even in those days. He took it with a smile. He was in the *NHL!*

Before his career was over, Phil Esposito became one of the highest-paid players in all of hockey.

Nothing, however, was very easy for Espo. The Black Hawks sent him to a minor league club for some "seasoning." It was 1964 before he was finally called up to the Black Hawks.

Then Esposito didn't do all that well. The Chicago fans didn't seem to like him. He didn't get along too well with the Chicago star center, Stan Mikita.

Esposito didn't think they were paying him enough by then, either.

The coach didn't think he was trying as hard as he could. The sports writers made fun of him. They thought he was clumsy compared to Mikita, their star. But Espo *was* trying and he was scoring. For the first time in history, the Hawks finished in first place in 1966–67.

Then the Hawks lost in the first round of the playoffs. The team was embarrassed. Phil was traded to the Boston Bruins.

Boston! Of *all* places. At that time, the Bruins were the worst team in the league. From the top, Espo had been sent to the bottom. He was bitter and angry.

But Boston and the fans of the Bruins welcomed him with open arms. They knew they *needed* Esposito. They even made him the assistant captain on the team. Such a welcome was a new experience for Phil Esposito. He began to change his mind about the Boston Bruins.

"OK," he said to himself, "they're treating me right. I'll show them. I'll show the Black Hawks. I'll show *everybody* who Phil Esposito is."

And he *did!* By the middle of the season, the

Bruins were tied for the lead with the Black Hawks. The team had made a complete turn-around. Phil Esposito was responsible. He kept nagging his teammates to try harder.

In 1968, Tony Esposito became the goalie for the Montreal Canadiens. Often the two teams, the Bruins and the Canadiens, played each other. Phil Esposito was proud of his kid brother, Tony. He told everybody Tony was one of the best goalies in the NHL.

But he laughed when they kidded him about "going easy" on his kid brother. When they played each other, Tony was just another goalie trying to keep him from scoring. He was just another enemy player in the way of a goal.

The Boston Bruins had another player who was fast becoming a legend in hockey at that time. His name was Bobby Orr. He became one of the greatest defensemen in the history of hockey. He was also one of the great scorers in the game. Seldom do the two go together.

But even Bobby Orr was not scoring like Phil Esposito. Espo would park in the slot and fire in goal after goal. He was becoming another of pro hockey's scoring machines.

In the 1968–69 season, he finally hit the top. Esposito was awarded the Art Ross Trophy for the most points scored in a season. He had scored 49 goals and 77 assists for a grand total of 126 points. It was a new NHL scoring record. He was also awarded the Hart Memorial Trophy as the league's most valuable player. That same season his teammate Orr won the Norris Trophy for being the best defenseman in the NHL.

To get an award for yourself is fine, but the dream of every hockey player is for his team to win the Stanley Cup. It was just a little silver cup back in 1893 when Lord Stanley donated it. It was given to the winner of an amateur game in Canada. The winning team was the Montreal A.A.A. The trophy cost Lord Stanley only 10 guineas. That's about $50.

Today the cup is a little worse for the wear. It is much larger, too. It stands much taller than before. Collars have been added around the bottom to make room for the names of new winners to be engraved. The Stanley Cup is one of the most wanted trophies in all of sports.

For his team to win the cup is the highest moment of any hockey player's career. With the solid scoring of Phil Esposito, the Bruins won it in 1970. They beat the Black Hawks in the semifinal round. They won four games to none in the best-of-seven series to become the Eastern Division champs.

The Chicago goalie was Tony Esposito. Tony was saddened by the loss. But Phil insisted that his brother had played well. It was just that the Bruins were *ready*. They really *wanted* the Stanley Cup.

So they played the weaker St. Louis Blues' team in the final round. The Blues were the Western Division champs. The Bruins won easily, four games in a row. They were at the top of hockey. They were the Stanley Cup champions!

They won the famous cup again in the 1971–72 season. They were a powerhouse. With Esposito and Orr, they had become the most feared team in hockey. They were called the Big Bad Bruins by fans and the press. They were *tough*.

Phil Esposito set a new scoring record. This one stood until 1982, when Wayne Gretzky finally broke it.

The Bruins were on their way to a third Stanley

Cup the following season, 1972–73. But Phil Esposito was injured in the playoffs. His knee muscles were torn and he was out of hockey for the rest of the season. The Bruins lost.

At the party at the end of the season, some players sneaked into Phil's hospital room. They rolled him, bed and all, out of the hospital. They took him to the party for the team. Hours later they brought him back. The doctors and nurses had been looking all over for him.

A shocking thing happened to Espo during the 1975–76 season. He was the leader of the Bruins and one of the all-time scorers in hockey. He was happy in Boston.

So everybody was surprised when the team traded Espo to the New York Rangers. Often such trades do not make sense to fans, but they happen anyhow. Esposito was unhappy with the trade, too. He thought he would be a Bruin for the rest of his career. He didn't want to be traded. He didn't understand.

But finally he got used to his new team.

Then he was the old Espo again. He would camp in the slot and shove in the garbage goals.

Espo (*far right*) waits in the slot for the puck to come in as the goalie gets his stick on a forward too near his territory.

The goalie would save a goal. The rebound would pop out. And there would be Espo to shove it back in for another score.

New York loved him. For five more years, until 1980, he played with the Rangers. Once the team went all the way to the Stanley Cup finals. This is something very few teams do. They were beaten by the mighty Montreal Canadiens.

Finally, Phil Esposito retired. He felt he was getting too old to play. He is in the record book on a number of pages. He had the most goals in one season (76) until Wayne Gretzky finally broke the record in 1982. He had the most seasons with 40 or more goals (7). He had the most career hat tricks, or three goals in one game (32).

Espo was best at short ranges. Most of his goals were scored within a few inches to a few feet from

The poor goalie doesn't know which way to turn with Espo out to his left and the puck surely coming in.

the net. Many of them were off rebounds. Or off other players. Or off other parts of his own body. They didn't appear planned, but they were.

Espo was willing to wait that extra split second before shooting. He placed the pucks in the net where he wanted them. He put them where the goalie wasn't.

Garbage goals?

Another great hockey player, Wayne Cashman, explained. "There's no such thing as a garbage goal. You never hear anyone in baseball say that was a bad home run, do you? What Espo had was a knack around the net, a real skill. I'll tell you, he scored a lot of very *pretty* goals, too."

Phil Esposito is one of the greatest super-champions in all of pro hockey. He is still seen around hockey games. Especially those of the New York Rangers. Espo is the "color man" working with the play-by-play radio announcer.

Almost certainly he will sooner or later be hired by some NHL team as a coach or even general manager. It is only a matter of time.

INDEX

Boldface page numbers refer to photos

James Norris Memorial
Trophy, 64–65, 111

Kings. *See* Los Angeles
Kings

Lady Byng Trophy, 34
Lafleur, Guy, 23, 32,
35, 43, **88,** 89–101,
89, 92, 96-97
Lafleur, Lise, 95
Lester B. Pearson Me-
morial Award, 35
Libby, Bill, 70, 100–01
Liut, Mike, **2,** 38
Los Angeles Kings, 33,
34, 38, 39

Maple Leafs. *See* To-
ronto Maple Leafs
Meloche, Gilles, 18
Mikita, Stan, 108, 109
Montreal A.A.A., 111
Montreal Canadiens,
26, 32, 35, 38, 90,
91–93, 95, 99, 114

New York Islanders, 13,
14, 15, 18–19, 21,

22, 26, 60, 64,
69–71, 72, 73
New York Rangers,
113–14, 116
Nordiques. *See* Quebec
Nordiques
Norris Memorial Tro-
phy, 64–65, 111

Oilers. *See* Edmonton
Oilers
Olympic Games, Lake
Placid, 1980, 75–78
Orr, Bobby, **4-5,** 5, 65,
72, 110, 111, 112
Orr, Frank, 99

Palmer, Rob, 38
Park, Brad, 99
Pearson Memorial
Award, 35
Philadelphia Flyers, 70
Potvin, Armand, 63
Potvin, Bob, 63, 64
Potvin, Denis, **ii, 60,**
61–73, **61, 66-67,**
71
Potvin, Jean, 63, 64